ADVENTURES IN AMERICA

Student Notebook

WRITTEN BY:
ANGELA BLAU

Copyright

Summary of Student Notebook

USA Blank Map

Each week, have your student color the particular state or states that you have read about. You may choose to use different colors to easily distinguish each state. After your student has completed coloring that week's state, point to previously learned states and review the names and locations.

Coloring Pages

Each week has one related coloring page. After your student has colored the page, you may ask them to give the picture a caption. Periodically, look back over completed pages as review.

Narration Pages

This blank page can be used for recording oral narrations given from the week's history reading, Read Aloud or reader. After you write your student's narration on the lines, your child can illustrate the box above however they like.

Copywork Pages

For each week, you will need to write a model of the copywork sentence onto handwriting paper for them to copy into the notebook. The box above can be used to illustrate the sentence or to paste a picture of the week's hands-on activity or craft.

State Pages

These pages are for recording the state's abbreviation, capital and nickname. After looking at the state in *Smart About the Fifty States*, have your student point to where the capital should be on the blank map. Let them place a foil star sticker (or draw a star) in that location. They may wish to color the state outline map, and they could even add rivers and other geographical details if they are interested. The blank rectangle at the top of each page is for a sticker of the state flag. These are inexpensively available at www.amazon.com, www.rainbowresource.com and various education supply stores.

Table of Contents

The United States of America

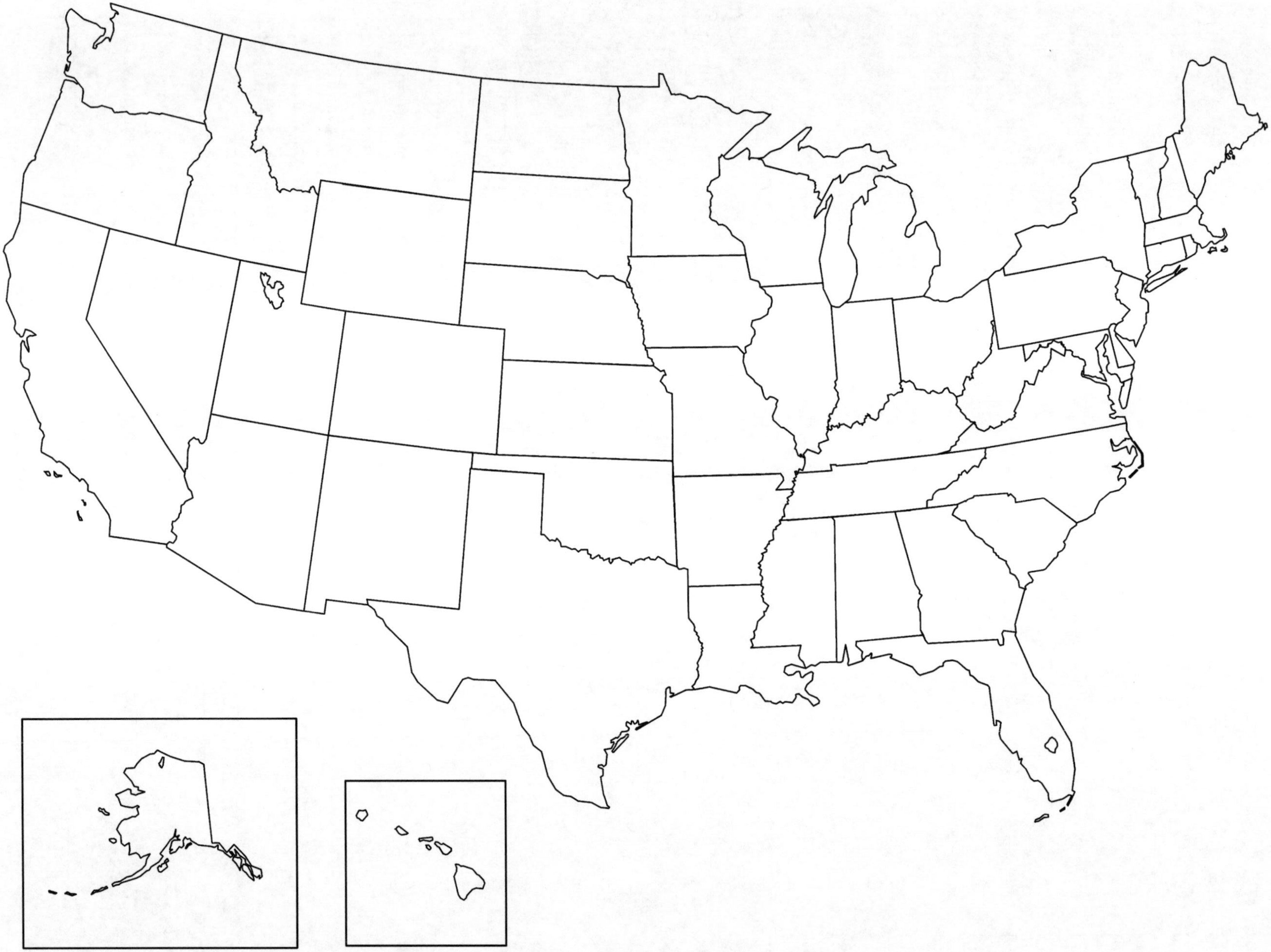

Adventures in America Week 1 Copywork

DELAWARE

Capital: _____ Abbreviation: _____

Nickname: _____

Something I thought interesting: _____

_____

_____

PENNSYLVANIA

Flag Sticker

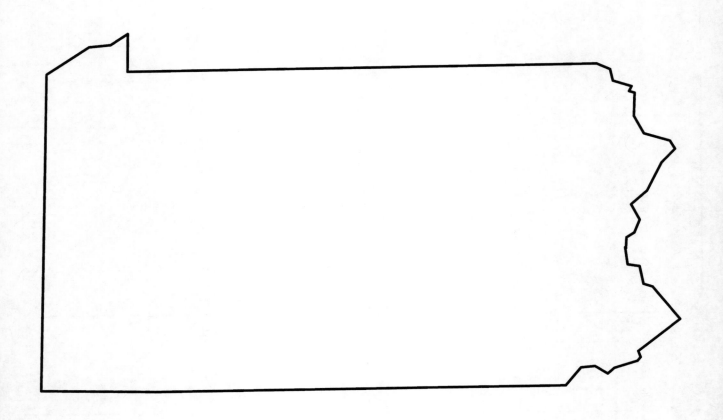

Capital: _____ Abbreviation: _____

Nickname: _____

Something I thought interesting: _____

_____

_____

NEW JERSEY

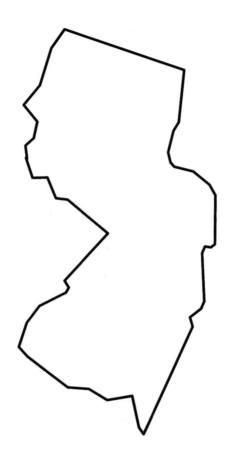

Capital: _____   Abbreviation: _____

Nickname: _____

Something I thought interesting: _____

_____

_____

GEORGIA

Capital: _____   Abbreviation: _____

Nickname: _____

Something I thought interesting: _____

_____

_____

18

CONNECTICUT

Capital: _____ Abbreviation: _____

Nickname: _____

Something I thought interesting: _____

_____

_____

19

MASSACHUSETTS

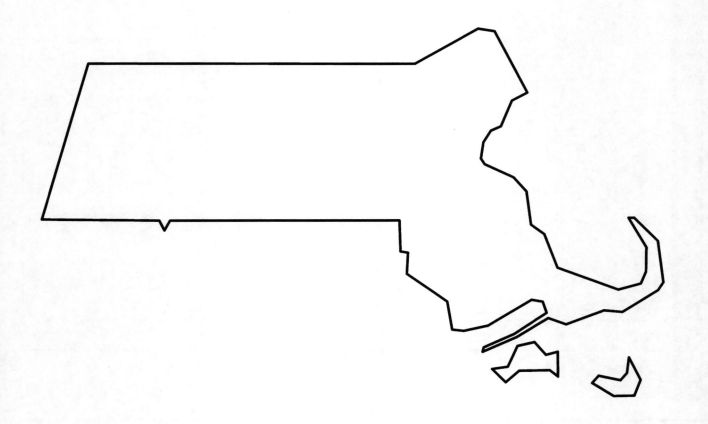

Capital: _____ Abbreviation: _____

Nickname: _____

Something I thought interesting: _____

_____

_____

Adventures in America Week 6 Copywork

MARYLAND

Flag Sticker

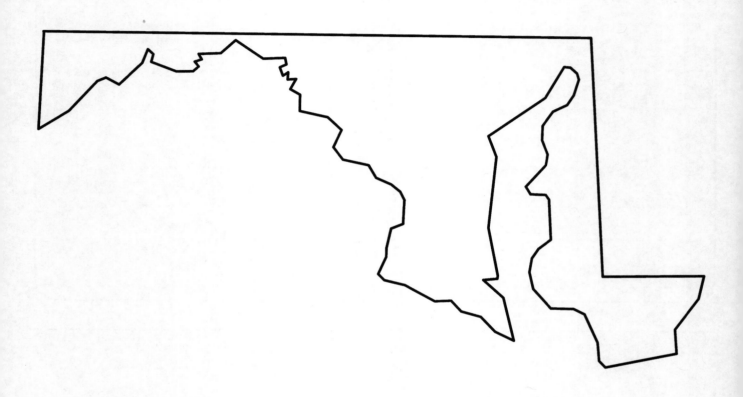

Capital: _____   Abbreviation: _____

Nickname: _____

Something I thought interesting: _____

_____

_____

28

SOUTH CAROLINA

Flag Sticker

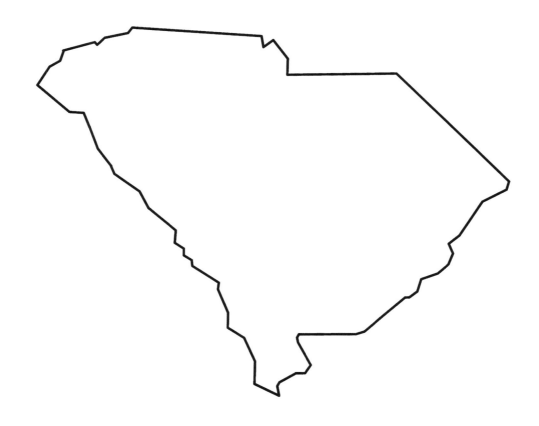

Capital: _____ Abbreviation: _____

Nickname: _____

Something I thought interesting: _____

_____

_____

NEW HAMPSHIRE

Flag Sticker

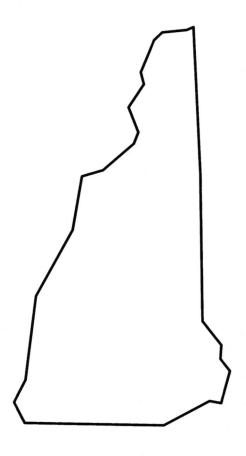

Capital: _____   Abbreviation: _____

Nickname: _____

Something I thought interesting: _____

_____

_____

34

Adventures in America Week 8 Copywork

VIRGINIA

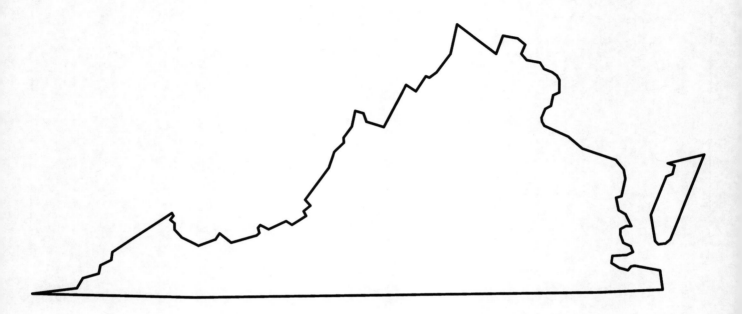

Capital: _____ Abbreviation: _____

Nickname: _____

Something I thought interesting: _____

_____

_____

NEW YORK

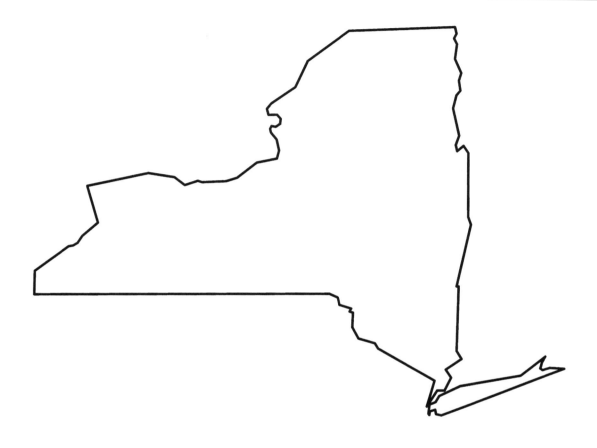

Capital: _____   Abbreviation: _____

Nickname: _____

Something I thought interesting: _____

_____

_____

Adventures in America Week 9 Copywork

NORTH CAROLINA

Flag Sticker

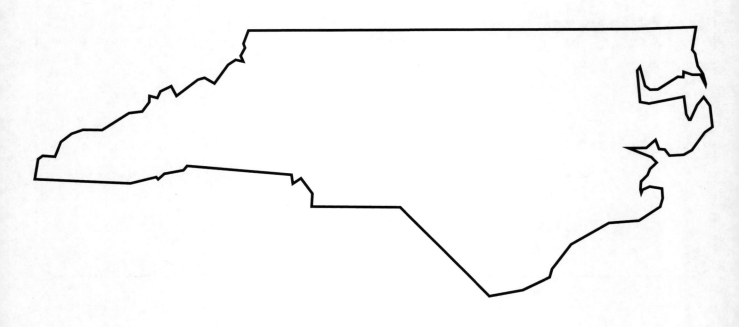

Capital: _____   Abbreviation: _____

Nickname: _____

Something I thought interesting: _____

_____

_____

RHODE ISLAND

Flag Sticker

Capital: _____ Abbreviation: _____

Nickname: _____

Something I thought interesting: _____

_____

_____

VERMONT

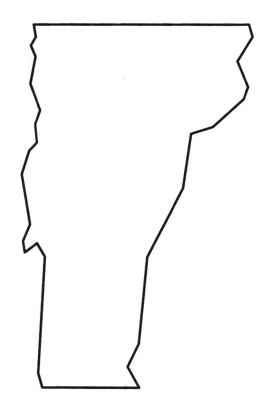

Capital: _____ Abbreviation: _____

Nickname: _____

Something I thought interesting: _____

_____

_____

KENTUCKY

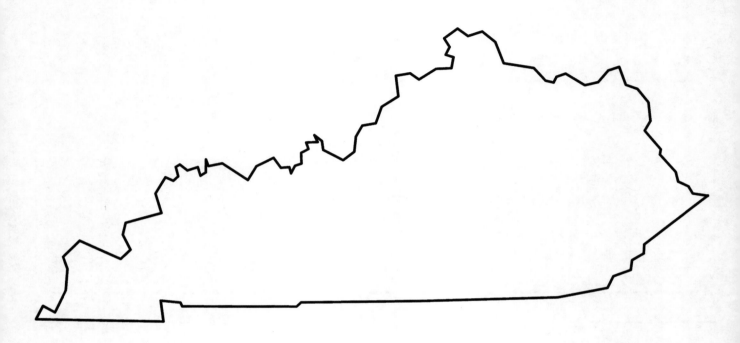

Capital: _____   Abbreviation: _____

Nickname: _____

Something I thought interesting: _____

_____

_____

TENNESSEE

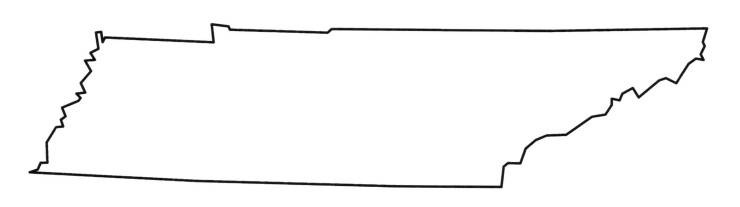

Capital: _____ Abbreviation: _____

Nickname: _____

Something I thought interesting: _____

_____

_____

Adventures in America Week 12 Narration

58

OHIO

Capital: _____   Abbreviation: _____

Nickname: _____

Something I thought interesting: _____

_____

_____

LOUISIANA

Capital: _____   Abbreviation: _____

Nickname: _____

Something I thought interesting: _____

_____

_____

INDIANA

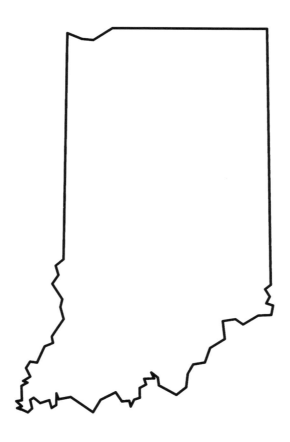

Capital: _____   Abbreviation: _____

Nickname: _____

Something I thought interesting: _____

_____

_____

MISSISSIPPI

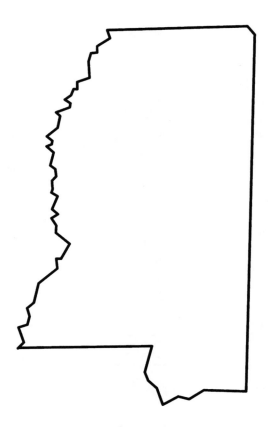

Capital: _____   Abbreviation: _____

Nickname: _____

Something I thought interesting: _____

_____

_____

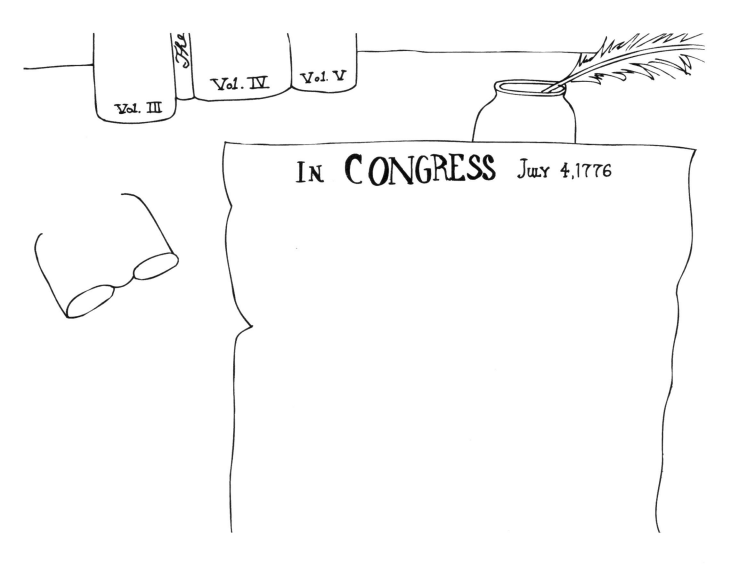

Vol. III

Vol. IV

Vol. V

IN CONGRESS   July 4, 1776

ILLINOIS

Capital: _____   Abbreviation: _____

Nickname: _____

Something I thought interesting: _____

_____

_____

ALABAMA

Capital: _____ Abbreviation: _____

Nickname: _____

Something I thought interesting: _____

_____

_____

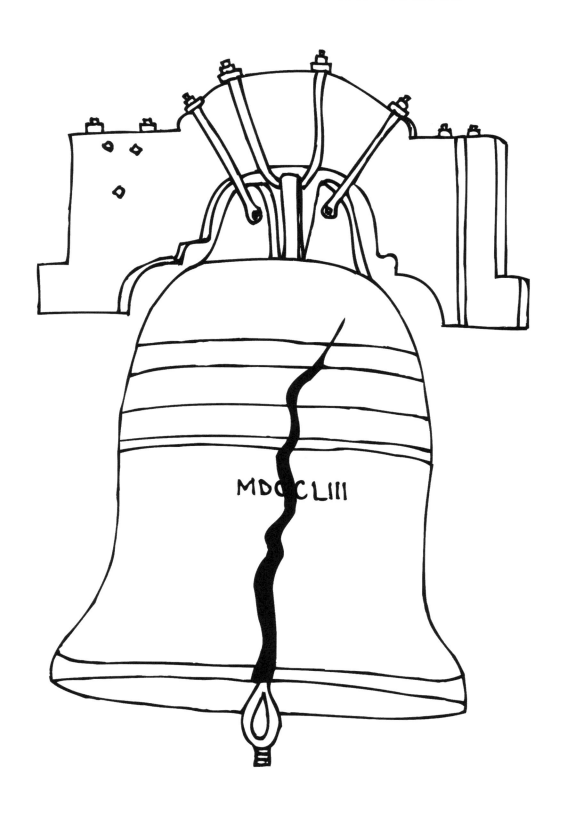

MAINE

Capital: _____   Abbreviation: _____

Nickname: _____

Something I thought interesting: _____

_____

_____

MISSOURI

Capital: _____ Abbreviation: _____

Nickname: _____

Something I thought interesting: _____

_____

_____

ARKANSAS

Capital: _____ Abbreviation: _____

Nickname: _____

Something I thought interesting: _____

_____

_____

Adventures in America Week 18 Narration

MICHIGAN

Flag Sticker

Capital: _____   Abbreviation: _____

Nickname: _____

Something I thought interesting: _____

_____

_____

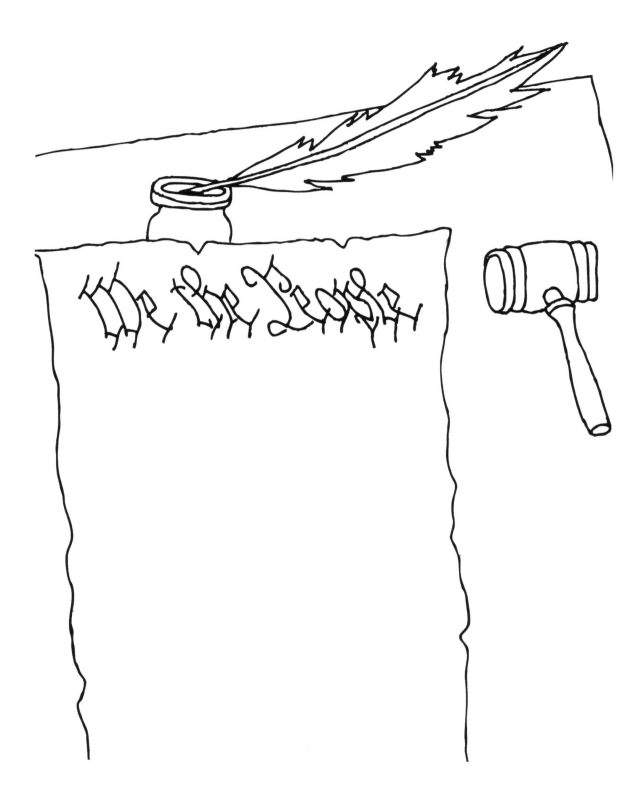

FLORIDA

Capital: _____   Abbreviation: _____

Nickname: _____

Something I thought interesting: _____

_____

_____

TEXAS

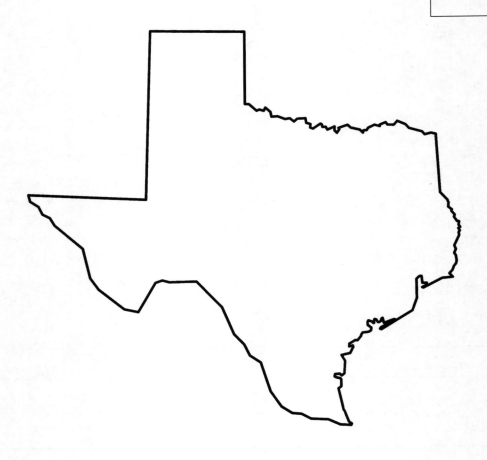

Capital: _____   Abbreviation: _____

Nickname: _____

Something I thought interesting: _____

_____

_____

IOWA

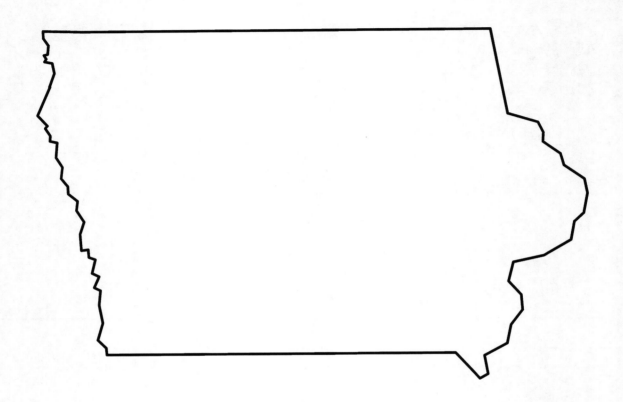

Capital: _____   Abbreviation: _____

Nickname: _____

Something I thought interesting: _____

_____

_____

WISCONSIN

Capital: _____ Abbreviation: _____

Nickname: _____

Something I thought interesting: _____

_____

_____

CALIFORNIA

Flag Sticker

Capital: _____ Abbreviation: _____

Nickname: _____

Something I thought interesting: _____

_____

_____

MINNESOTA

Capital: _____ Abbreviation: _____

Nickname: _____

Something I thought interesting: _____

_____

_____

OREGON

Flag Sticker

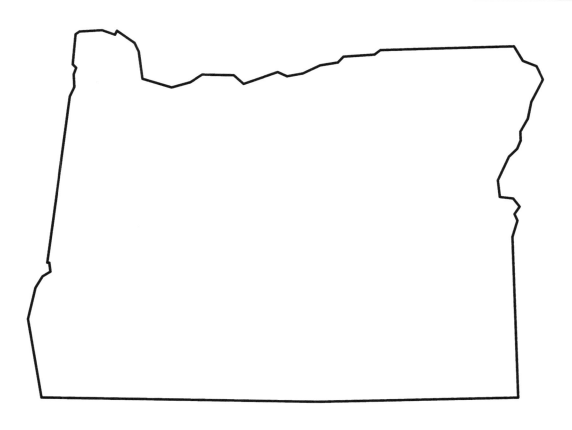

Capital: _____ Abbreviation: _____

Nickname: _____

Something I thought interesting: _____

_____

_____

113

KANSAS

Capital: _____ Abbreviation: _____

Nickname: _____

Something I thought interesting: _____

_____

_____

Adventures in America Week 25 Copywork

WEST VIRGINIA

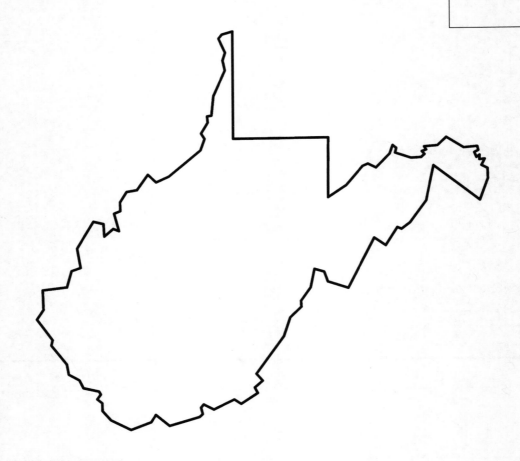

Capital: _____   Abbreviation: _____

Nickname: _____

Something I thought interesting: _____

_____

_____

Adventures in America Week 26 Copywork

NEVADA

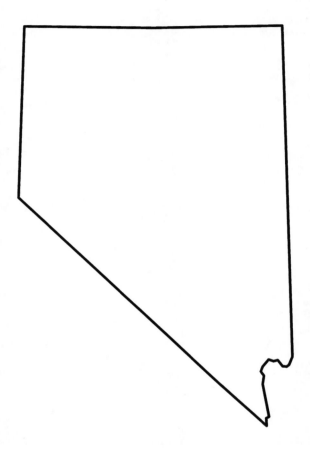

Capital: _____   Abbreviation: _____

Nickname: _____

Something I thought interesting: _____

_____

_____

NEBRASKA

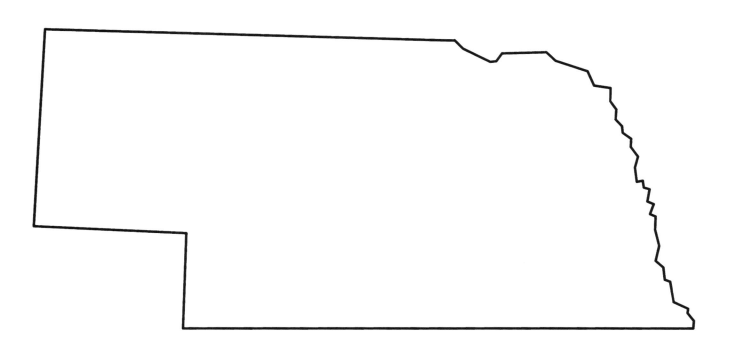

Capital: _____ Abbreviation: _____

Nickname: _____

Something I thought interesting: _____

_____

_____

COLORADO

Flag Sticker

Capital: _____ Abbreviation: _____

Nickname: _____

Something I thought interesting: _____

_____

_____

NORTH DAKOTA

Flag Sticker

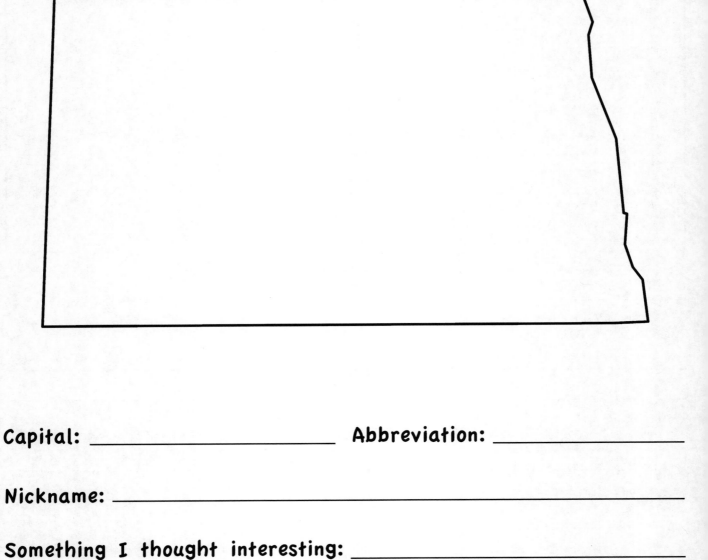

Capital: _____ Abbreviation: _____

Nickname: _____

Something I thought interesting: _____

_____

_____

SOUTH DAKOTA

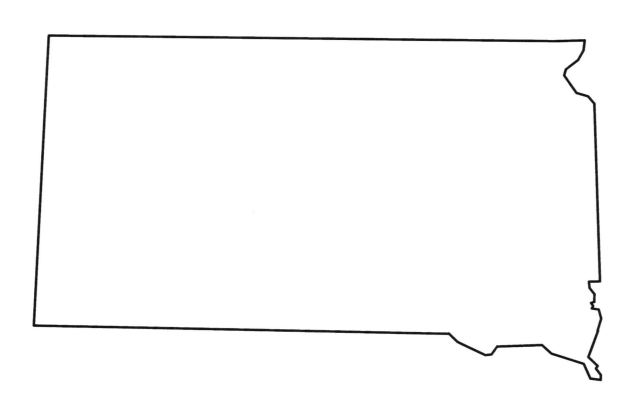

Capital: _____   Abbreviation: _____

Nickname: _____

Something I thought interesting: _____

_____

_____

137

Adventures in America Week 29 Copywork

MONTANA

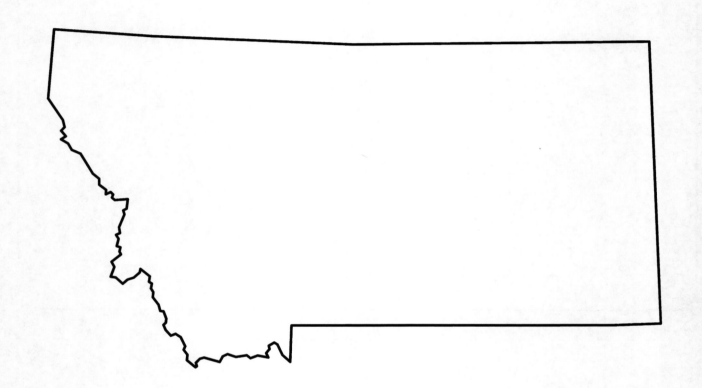

Capital: _____   Abbreviation: _____

Nickname: _____

Something I thought interesting: _____

_____

_____

142

WASHINGTON

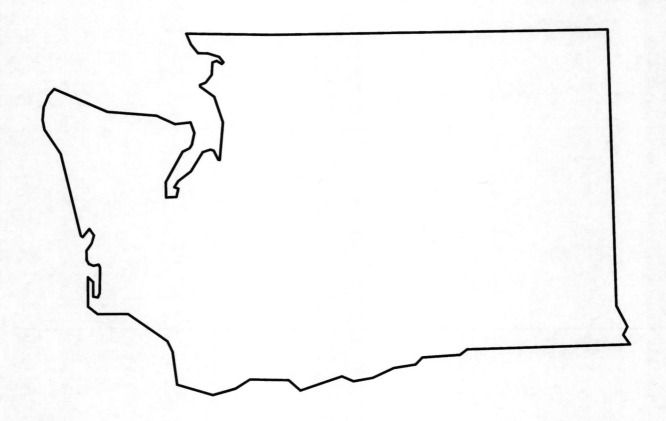

Capital: _____ Abbreviation: _____

Nickname: _____

Something I thought interesting: _____

_____

_____

IDAHO

Capital: _____   Abbreviation: _____

Nickname: _____

Something I thought interesting: _____

_____

_____

Adventures in America Week 31 Narration

WYOMING

Capital: _____   Abbreviation: _____

Nickname: _____

Something I thought interesting: _____

_____

_____

UTAH

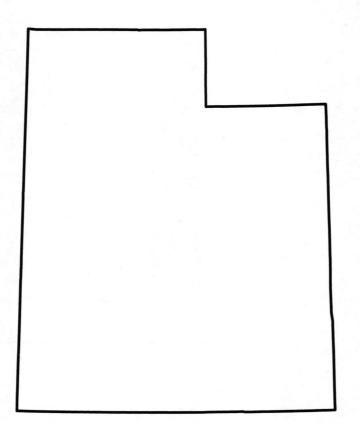

Capital: _____   Abbreviation: _____

Nickname: _____

Something I thought interesting: _____

_____

_____

OKLAHOMA

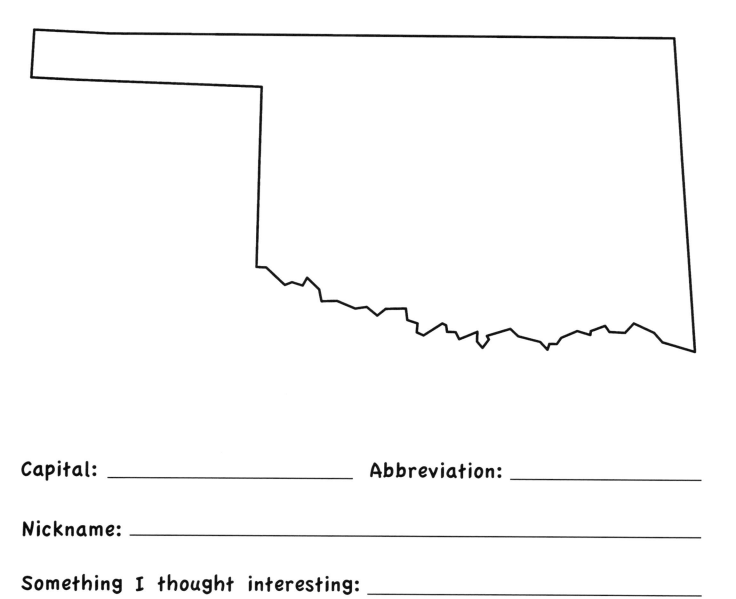

Capital: _____   Abbreviation: _____

Nickname: _____

Something I thought interesting: _____

_____

_____

NEW MEXICO

Flag Sticker

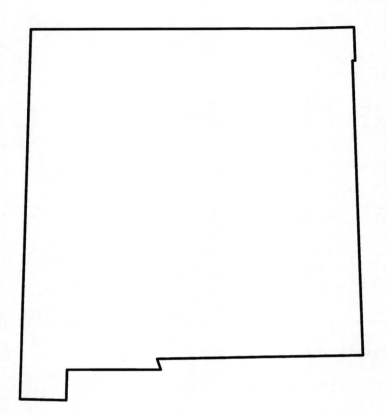

Capital: _____ Abbreviation: _____

Nickname: _____

Something I thought interesting: _____

_____

_____

Adventures in America Week 34 Copywork

ARIZONA

Flag Sticker

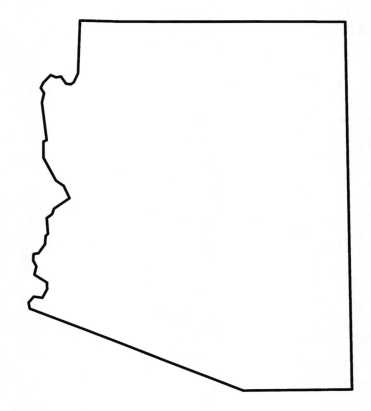

Capital: _____ Abbreviation: _____

Nickname: _____

Something I thought interesting: _____

_____

_____

166

ALASKA

Capital: _____ Abbreviation: _____

Nickname: _____

Something I thought interesting: _____

_____

_____

HAWAII

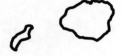

Capital: _____ Abbreviation: _____

Nickname: _____

Something I thought interesting: _____

_____

_____

172

Adventures in America Week 36 Narration

MY STATE

My State: _____   State Bird: _____

State Flower: _____

State Motto: _____

State Nickname: _____

Physical Features: _____

_____

_____

_____

My State is Interesting Because: _____

_____

_____

_____

_____